"If you never imagine that haiku could be funny, you haven't read Laura Martin's haiku. The queen of zombie haiku, Martin's *Haiku for the Undead* is a delight, starting with simple poems in the classic form, then widening into longer pieces of chained haiku—many humorous, some reflecting on life in the suburbs, politics, menopause and the pandemic. Perhaps most delightful are the long titles that precede the tightly composed poetic gems, each one meant to be read aloud, tasted, chuckled over and savored."

—Jan Haag, editor Amherst Writers & Artists Press

"After reading Laura Martin's *Haiku for the Undead*, I'm still not sure I believe in Zombies, but maybe I do. Martin talks about them in such a sweet way they have to be real. She made me smile, think about things, wonder how many pieces I'm made of, and where they came from. Martin hides no hearts; she simply teases the reader of all we should know. She'll leave you feeling warm, understood, and glad you spent some time with her—I do."

—Bill Gainer, author of *A True Story (Used Poems, 2003 – 2021)*

"You think you know zombies? You think you know haiku? Think again, friend. One by one, these mutant three-line creatures will take, as Emily Dickinson famously said of poetry, "the top of your head off." I've always been amazed at how Laura Martin's poems make me laugh and think at the same time. She cracks you up, and then she brings you right back to earth. For one, here's "The Lonely Zombie:"

> *Her desire for*
> *a wild heart overlooked the*
> *fact he had no brains.*

Buy this book. I think it casts a curse on those who touch it and don't."

—Bob Stanley, Sacramento Poet Laureate 2009 – 2012

"Delightfully cheeky, hilarious, and poignant, Laura Martin's work of zombie haikus is a mash-up of clever fun. The perfect unique gift for the lover of the Undead!"

—Katie McCleary, best-selling author and podcast host of NPR's *The Drive*

HAIKU FOR THE UNDEAD

(FROM THE "ALL HIGH, NO KU—POETRY UNDER THE INFLUENCE" COLLECTION)

LAURA MARTIN

Gasconade Press

Belle, MO

Copyright © Laura Martin, 2022

First Edition 1 3 5 7 9 10 8 6 4 2

ISBN: 978-1-958182-19-2

LCCN: 2022944486

Author photo: Laura Martin

Cover and title page image: Robert Hansen

Publication credits:

"Ganja Zombie," "Commitment Zombies," "Sex Zombie" and "The Zombie Goes to the Halloween Party, Dateless" previously published in *Sacramento News & Review;* Vol. 24, Issue 28; 10/25/12

Chapter I previously published in *Haiku for the Undead;* Poems-for-All #1111; 2012, 2014

Chapter II previously published in *Haiku for the Undead II— Zombie Apocalyptic Dance Party!;* Poems-for-All #1248; 2014

Chapter III previously published in *Haiku for the Undead III— Suburbia Graveyard at the End of the Cul-de-sac;* Poems-for-All #1353; 2015

Chapter IV previously published in *Haiku for the Undead IV— Attack of the 50-foot Cluster B;* Poems-for-All #1541; 2016

Chapter V previously published in *Haiku for the Undead V— #RESIST: Deconstructing the Narcissistic Wet Dream;* Poems-for-All #1712; 2017

Chapter VI previously published in *Haiku for the Undead VI— My Uterus is a Roller Derby Queen;* Poems-for-All #1850; 2019

TABLE OF CONTENTS

Table of Contents

I
Haiku for the Undead / 1

II
Zombie Apocalyptic Dance Party / 9

III
Suburbia Graveyard at the End of the Cul-de-sac / 17

IV
Attack of the 50-foot Cluster B / 25

V
#RESIST: Deconstructing the Narcissistic Wet Dream / 35

VI
My Uterus is a Roller Derby Queen / 45

VII
Welcome to the Post-Pandemic Resocialization Project / 57

In a small Northern California town sometimes all there is to do is have an imagination

You can take the girl
out of Weed, but never the
Weed out of the girl.

I

Haiku for the Undead

Ganja Zombie

They smoked their brains out,
sloth'd to Mickey D's, ordered
large fries, extra salt.

The Valentine-less Zombie

She ate every piece
and walked around all day with
her heart box, empty.

Zombies in Love
Standing crotch to crotch,
tongue kissing hard in public—
strangers watch the show.

The Subtle Zombie
He tapped my shoulder,
politely opened my skull
and ate my think mush.

Commitment Zombies
One by one they both
consumed them all. Now they had
only each other.

Frankenstein, the Quilted Zombie
He asked her to dance.
She laughed at his two left feet
and his hands, all thumbs.

Sex Zombie
He finished first and
she laid there, still, not knowing
if they were done yet.

The Lonely Zombie
Her desire for
a wild heart overlooked the
fact he had no brains.

The Zombie Goes to the Halloween Party, Dateless

He shunned the costume
and everyone asked, *Who are
you supposed to be?*

II

Zombie Apocalyptic Dance Party

Too Many Meetings Make Jack a Dull Zombie

Your audience is
fading—too busy writing
poems, grocery lists.

Zombie Jack O' Lanterns Must Find New Jobs
Come November 1st

Carved faces helpless
in the gutter, mouths frozen
into shriveled screams.

**Social Network Zombie Floats Around
in the Digital Abyss**
Stupid Facebook friend
never comments on my wall—
Unfriend her tonight!

The Jilted Zombie
Erased completely
from his cell phone, no longer
caring if she calls.

**Gov'ment Worker Zombies Power Walk Around
Capitol, Straight Up Noon**

Brown slacks, tennis shoes,
cheap shades, ugly hats—each name
swinging from a neck.

Ladder Climber Zombie Finally Hits Glass Ceiling

Brains got her nowhere
fast, so she swapped them out for
fake smiles, faker parts.

Blind Date at the Zombie Apocalyptic Dance Party

Jaws dropped—couldn't take
their eyes off each other. Danced
'til their legs fell off.

Same Ol' Zombie Middle Management Blah Blah Blah

Great work if you can
get it—late nights, squelched dreams and
no brains required.

Zombie Boss Holds 9th Staff Meeting of the Week

Love the way he'll push
opinions like something to
give a shit about.

Nicotine Junkie Zombies Roam Downtown Sacramento on Break

Each block, smokers plugged
with cancer pacifiers—
suck the butt of death.

Happy Zombie Jesus Day
My birthday fell on
Easter, and all I got was
an Easter basket.

Creative Zombie Gets a State Job
Surfed the net all day.
Saved 10 minutes of real work
for late afternoon.

III

Suburbia Graveyard at the
End of the Cul-de-sac

Drove There Specifically for Bathtub Caulk and a Putty Knife—Came Home with a New Low-Drip Sprinkler System, Paver Stones for the Driveway and New Motion-Sensor Lights for the Front Porch

Losing track of sun-
filled days we used to not spend
inside Home Depot.

Big Box is Slowly Boxing Us in One Half-Caf-Low-Foam-Double-Shot-Soy-Caramel Latte at a Time

Starbucks, Home Depot;
no reason to ever leave—
all we need is here.

**Romans 13:11–12—We're Not Religious by Any Means,
but Since Our House May Be a Little Bit Haunted,
We'll Take Any Advice We Can Get**
Just leave the lights on.
It's easier than cussing
out the ghosts all night.

**The Whole Neighborhood Has Turned into One Big
Suburbia Graveyard at the End of the Cul-de-sac**
Previous owners
enjoyed long lives. New buyers
enjoy the short sales.

King Size, Queen Size, Even Twin—Too Many Damn Thumbtack Holes to Ever Go Back on the Bed

Sheet curtains. No cash.
Settle for "Mid-Century
Modern Meth House" look.

That Moment You Realize You Can Spend Your Money Doing Something Way More Fun

Dream goal: Refurbish!
New goal: Make it look like a
really nice rental.

**They Ate Their Cake, Too, Then Complained
There Wasn't Enough Goddamn Cake**
Mad because lattes
got cold as they stood in line
inside Home Depot.

**Moved Six Months Ago and Too Tired to Deal With
All the Boxes Still Left to Unpack**
Bought house because of
back yard. Have eaten dinner
outside only once.

Excuse Me, but I Only Need One More of These in the "Aloha Tropical" Pattern. Do You Think You Have Any More in the Back?

Spent all weekend in
search of matching chair pads at
eight different Walmarts.

IV

Attack of the 50-foot Cluster B

Undedication:

You probably think
this haiku book is about
you, don't you? Don't you?

**Phase I: Idealization—Love Junkie Detonates a
Love Bomb During an Unprecedented Time of
Peace, Quiet and Calm**
She slid under his
skin without bothering to
first tap for a vein.

**Saran Wrap Girl Calls Him 10 Times a Day So He
Can Be the First One to Hear Her New Jokes**
She was clingy—like
rubbing-a-balloon-across-
your-pant-leg clingy.

**When the World Ends, I'll Meet You in Front of
the Gift Shop**
You're a lunatic!
said the freak magnet. Neither
one could pull away.

**Not Even Jesus Freakin'
Christ Can Help You Now**
You think he walks on
water, but really, he just
walks all over you.

Her Web Just Gets Bigger and Bigger as She Spins You Out of Control

Go ahead, dear—run,
spider said to ant. *Never
do I chase my food.*

Attack of the 50-ft Cluster B in My Bonnet Left the Perpetrator in Borderline Histrionics

I blew her cover—
she lost her shit. Still, I don't
feel we're even yet.

Sorry Not Sorry

That apology
felt like pulling belly fat
out of a zipper.

Wake Me Up When the Cheeto Dust Clears

Let's wish away this
election—raging Oompa
Loompa just a dream...

**NY Times Says Presidential Hopeful Has a Sad,
Lonely Life**
Don't feel sorry for
his sad life—his bigly hands
company enough.

**Phase III: Devaluation—When the Shitstorm Finally
Hits, You Better Hope You've Got
One Friend Left to Lend You a
Waterproof Jacket**
When will you learn? She's
not the life raft you think she
is—she's the sinking.

Phase III: Discard—If Silent Treatment is Golden, She Intends to Make You Rich

Crocodile tears fall
like pressed coal down her face, her
mask laid bare and drenched.

It's Called "Hoovering" Because They Eventually Come Back Around and Try to Suck You Back into Their Crazy—Starts Out Subtle and Slow, and You've Got to Protect Carefully Your Heart, Your Head and Mostly Your Back

Good advice: unlike,
unfriend, uncare, unfollow—
lather / rinse / repeat.

**Lucky You, to Embrace Change So Magnificently,
So Whole Heartedly, to Be So Normal, to Have
Such Confidence and Balance and Two Strong
Steady Feet to Land Upon—Look at Your Hands,
They Don't Even Tremble When You Read This**
It hurts to let go,
to unwind, to unclench the
tightly balled-up fist.

Flee the Triangulation
Stop. Breathe deep. Leap off
that corner assigned to you.
Unfurl your arms—fly.

V

#RESIST: Deconstructing the Narcissistic Wet Dream

You Have to Realize You Fell Asleep First Before You Can #staywoke

Never realized
you had a say? Your vote is
proof of ownership.

"#WeAreAltGov and we are not going anywhere"

Taxpayers' chorus
of voices rise: *We are here,*
you are not alone...

He Uses One Hand to Grab Them by the Pussy, the Other To Rub One Out in 140 Characters or Less

4 a.m. Twitter
fit—can't he just masturbate
like everyone else???

Tomato, Tomato; Potato, Potato; Impeachment, Impeachment

You say "covfefe"
I say "covfeefee"—let's just
call his whole term off!

Wait a Minute—Which One's the Puppet Again?

His twittertantrums
are getting quite stale—same ol'
shit—different toilet…

**Don the Con Releases his Flying Monkeys but
Couldn't See the Legal Forest Through the 1st
Amendment Trees**

45 gunned for
Alt_Immi; constitution
put him in his place.

"First they came for the scientists and the National Parks Services said, 'LOL, no' and went rogue..."
Smokey the Bear says:
Only YOU can prevent the
next apocalypse...

**"Yet Neither Do We Want to Fail to Hold Out the
Hope of Redemption..."**
Not the first devil
in the white house—first time he's
been so obvious...

You Can Forgive a Human for 'most Anything,
Except Having a Vagina…
How many hard-ons
have led to war? One dick match
after another…

Noah Doesn't Have Time for Your Liberal Snowflake
Tears—the Sky Is Growing Dark, the Clouds Are
Closing in and (if You Listen Real Close) the Birds
Aren't Even Singing Anymore
What did you expect?
You laughed as he built that ark,
scoffed at his rain dance…

**Cheeto Mussolini and The Orange Dust Manifesto
Orchestra present: A Winter Dance Party Night to
Remember**
Miller sways, Bannon
dips Kellyanne—they all dream
of a white Christmas...

**Some of my Favorite Writers Are Adjunct Professors by
Day, Nazi-Punchers by Night**
Who saw this coming?
Poets teaching us to breathe
through wet bandanas...

**When All This Blows Over, Maybe Kellyanne Will Find
a Nice Quiet Job Flipping Cue Cards for a Living**

Russian collusion?
Constitution solution
clears up confusion!

**Moochin' Mnuchin and his 24K Fort Knox Moonin'
Rendez-viewin'**

Flew south on our dime—
left ass cheek prints on top a
mountain of gold bars.

Deconstructing the Narcissistic Wet Dream
Call, write, stay woke, vote—
put on your pink pussy hat
and march, dammit, march!!!

#resist
Mad as hell? Call your
reps (202) 224
3121 now!

VI

My Uterus is a Roller Derby Queen

**My Uterus is a Roller Derby Queen—Kicked,
Punched, Shoved to the Ground Seven Times
(She Will Rise Up Eight)**

Ovaries clenched like
two mighty fists—she strikes back
in the voting booth.

**Someone Tell #45 That the "V" In "Vagina" Stands
for V-I-C-T-O-R-Y**

She'll run for mayor,
gov'nor, Congress—but she will
never run from YOU!

Making Grandpa Munster's Hair Great Again

This is it—the old
age of my youth. Let go the
dark! Embrace the gray!

Sunday, Bloody Sunday (and Monday and Tuesday and Wednesday and...)

Flooding so bad I
built an ark—christened it the
USS Tampax.

Hysteroscopy, Polypectomy, D&C, IUD at 49

Pierced, gutted—feeling
like a jack-o-lantern with
its insides scooped out.

Ode to a Small, Plastic Hormonal Pogo Stick Savior That Thins the Red Sea Lining and Eases the Flood (for the Next Five Years at Least)

Oh, soft, sacred piece
of plastic—you hang like a
Jesus in my womb...

My Mind is Not the Only Thing I'm Changing
Every 2 to 3 Hours
What's stronger than me?
Can you bleed 16 weeks and
not find yourself dead?

Snow White Reflects on Hitting Middle Age
I don't feel as old
as I look, she said to her
tired mirror face.

When the Ocean Won't Stop Bleeding and High Ground is Nowhere in Sight, You Might as Well Say Fuck It and Go Eat Yourself Some Chocolate and a Big Fat Juicy Steak

40 days now since
the eggs started jumping ship
off my body ark...

Of Course, I End Up Not Being as Fertile as I Once Thought

Small uterus? So
much life wasted stressing out
over birth control!

Insomnia is a Bitch
itch, ache, cough, thirst, twitch,
hot, cold, numb, race, worry, sweat,
heart, throat, jaw, clench... breathe...

**Tumor? Polyps? Menopause? Cancer? I Could Really
Use Wonder Woman's Golden Lasso About Now**
Transvaginal wand
of absolute truth will find
answers to it all.

**Awake, 3 a.m. Every Morning—the New
Normal for the Hormonal Abnormal**

Sun turns to moon, turns
to sun—each day blurs into
the day before it…

Nigh to 50 and Feeling Like a Teenager Again!

Stained jeans, stained bed sheets—
never thought I'd re-live those
bloody surprises.

My Pretend-Zen Self Flows With Life Easily and Effortlessly
Red raging hormone
logjam ride month after month
on white winged cotton.

Nobody Told Me There'd be Days Like These
WTF midlife!?!
Sneezing and peeing shouldn't
ever couple up!

**Mid-Life Menopausal Mood Swings Meet Me
in the Kitchen Late at Night (aka: The Refuge
of Chopping Carrots)**
Sink blade into hard
orange flesh—push 'til anger
meets the cutting board.

**Good Gawd How Many Eggs Could be Left at My
Age—Shouldn't They Have All Shriveled Up
by Now?**
Out! Out! Get out of
my body you unwanted
half-children, get out!

**Not Really Hot-Cold-Hot-Cold, but, Like
Springsteen, I'm on Fire All the Time**
Sheets soaked, pillow damp—
night sweats without the honor
of one good wet dream.

**Headline Reads: "You're Not Going Crazy:
Menopause Has Hijacked Your Brain"**
My mind, a hot air
popper desperate to pop
every last kernel.

VII

Welcome to the Post-Pandemic Resocialization Project

Can We Be a Constellation Now? One Massive Bear Hug Clinging to the Evening Sky? How Much Tighter Could I Have Possibly Wrapped My Arms Around You After Falling Out of Orbit This Year of Dread and Isolation?

If it hadn't been
for the bones, I would have thought
myself just dreaming.

Our Future Selves Will Look Back Fondly at This Dark Hovering Cloud of Impending Doom and Remember Each Silver Lining We Convinced Ourselves to Be True

Remember that time
we all flew back into our
nests at once? Weird, huh?

**Outlined In Zuzu Port, Filled with Tarte Envy Matte,
Lusciously Topped Off with Careful Paint Strokes of
Gabriel Vino De Amour**

Old lip brush caked in
red—small remnants of what I
used to care about…

**Never Learned to Make Sourdough Bread—Too Busy
Praying Lyle Lovett and I Both Live Long Enough for
Me to See Him Again**

Can't wait for the day
me and that pony do some
cartwheels on his boat.

**Don't Let Anyone Tell You That It's Not OK to
Hold Your Breath When You've Grown Used to
Having All This Air Only to Yourself**
Wasn't that fun, the
three hot minutes of mask-free
life we got last spring?

**When We Rise Up from the Dead of This, You
Bring the Bread and the Water Unwalked Upon,
and I'll Bring the Bottle of Wine and Make Sure
There is Plenty of Fish for Everyone**
I miss worrying
about whether or not you
liked the meal I made.

Will We Still Recognize Each Other When We Remove the Cloth From the Holes on Our Face and Let Our Minds Flow Free on the Air We Share Between Us?

I know you now from
eyes up—fogged glasses, muffled
laughter, sterile wipes

gloved hands, incessant
headline reading, Lysol spray,
thermometer, this

strange gray silhouette
of you and I standing one
fresh-dug grave apart.

Tolerance For Bullshit, Patience for Stupidity, Resignation for Apathy, and My Underwear—This Pandemic Keeps Adding to the List of Things I Don't Fold Anymore

Figured my panties
always in a bunch—might as
well leave them that way.

Middle Of August, Broken Ceiling Fan, Too Much COVID Going Around to Get It Fixed, So I Wake Up Hot Like a Bruce Springsteen "I'm On Fire" Radio Sing-Along

This isn't really
how I pictured waterbeds
coming back in style…

I Knew It Was Serious—That Everyone Thought We Were All Going to Die—When Not Even the Name-Brand Stuff Could Be Found

I knew we were fucked
when the good TP flew off
grocery store shelves first.

Welcome to the Post-Pandemic Resocialization Project

How will we greet each
other when this is over?
A giant bear hug?

A warm handshake? High
fives all around? Will there be
balloons or perhaps

a parade? Shall we
wear our finest or will pants
still be optional?

Kill Both Birds, Keep the Rock Safe
and Deep Inside Your Pocket

I think maybe I
went insane during lockdown
and it just hasn't

caught up to me yet—
I have to admit I miss
the empty roads, the

steady hum of tires
rolling along shunned highways
heading to nowhere,

blinkers (optional),
gliding on empty bridges,
drifting lane to lane—

speed limits (merely
suggestions), no metering
at the onramps, the

offramp dismounts smooth
like room temperature butter—
not a cop in sight.

Laura Martin grew up in the small Northern California lumber town of Weed and started writing as soon as she could figure out how to hold a pencil in her chubby little fingers. Her work has appeared in publications such as *Late Peaches: Poems by Sacramento Poets, Gasconade Review, River Dog Zine, Peregrine,* and *Poems-For-All.* She has won several awards for her poetry and fronts The Soft Offs—a seven-piece spoken word music ensemble that takes the written word from page to stage.

Acknowledgments:

I may be the storyteller, but it takes one hell of a village to not lose your mind. THANK YOU to:

My partner (and favorite captive audience) Chris Musci who moved mountains and wrangled cats so I could do my thing. I love you. Without your help I would be way more insane than I already am...

John Dorsey and Jason Ryberg for this incredible opportunity through Gasconade Press to publish my first book and their patience and guidance as I stumbled along...

Robert Hansen whose "Poems for All" tiny book project (poems-for-all.com) is the reason this haiku collection exists. Robert published the first Haiku for the Undead tiny book in 2012 and I never thought I'd write more than the first handful, but here we are six tiny books (and counting!) later. Thank you for your graciousness in letting me be a part of your tiny book project—it's meant the world to me...

Jan Haag who has lovingly guided me and countless others to take a deep breath and just write; the "Team Haag" writing tribe who has listened to a gazillion of my crazy stories for more than a decade and keeps encouraging me to write more, especially Hilary Abramson, Dev Berger, Ed Cole, Linda Jackson Collins, Katie McCleary, Deborah Meltvedt, Krista Minard, April Peletta, Concepcion Tadeo and Pinky Wollerman...

My Thursday Night Writers—Cindy Domasky, Christie Domasky, Cheryle McLaughlin and Beth Suter who keep me sane at least one evening during the week...

The Soft Offs (thesoftoffs.com)—my spoken word band comprised of my partner Chris Musci, Bill McFall, Anthony Lucero, Ken Rabiroff, Tim Tucker and Greg Willett who've set many of my stories (and the first chapter of this book) to music—you guys make MOETRY so much fun...

Bill Gainer and his "Red Alice's Poetry Emporium" series at Shine café where my poetry peeps and I cut our teeth at open mic back in the day (thanks for letting us take over the blue couch Rena Davonne!); Bob Stanley, Stuart Canton and all the Sacramento Poetry Center peeps; Lob Instagon, Art Luna and Luna's Cafe, 916 Ink, Allan Ferreira and his "Night Roots" show on KFOK.org, and Dr. Andy Jones and the Davis poetry series...

My brother-from-another-mother Phillip Hight (I'll give you $10 if you can find the phrase I borrowed from you in this book), Angela Caldwell (artist/therapist/friend), Richard Schmidt (my favorite photographer), Kat Spence and Penny Tremper (mahalo, aloha wau iā 'oe); Susan Davis, John Ewing and Veronica Espinoza for their good fresh eyes; and #AltGov and #AltFam (keep up the good trouble my frens)...

Dave Iribarne, Sherri Goldberg, Carolyn Ralston—how I wish y'all were still here to see this.

This project was made possible, in part, by generous support from the Osage Arts Community.

Osage Arts Community provides temporary time, space and support for the creation of new artistic works in a retreat format, serving creative people of all kinds — visual artists, composers, poets, fiction and nonfiction writers. Located on a 152-acre farm in an isolated rural mountainside setting in Central Missouri and bordered by ¾ of a mile of the Gasconade River, OAC provides residencies to those working alone, as well as welcoming collaborative teams, offering living space and workspace in a country environment to emerging and mid-career artists. For more information, visit us at www.osageac.org

Osage Arts Community